LOC LOVE

BY JASMINE MORALES

TABLE OF CONTENT

Locking your hair requires maintenance that can become very costly in salons. This book will explain how to grow and maintain healthy locs yourself at home. Locs have become very popular. There are a variety of reasons why people choose to lock their hair.

Fashion statement –

Simply wearing Locs is cool to some.

Many are just copying athletes and musician who wear them.

Versatility –

Dreadlocks can be styled in many ways. They can be worn up or down, straight or curly or even colored. Some people like to wear beads, feathers and shells.

Maintenance -

Many people, mostly women find locs easier to maintain. Women who have bad experiences with heat and chemicals may choose to lock their hair dreadlocks do require careful maintenance.

Cultural statements – for many years having straight, long hair has been a high standard in society. Those who do not have naturally straight hair have to achieve straight hair with chemicals and heat.

Throughout the year's many people of African descent no longer feel they must meet the straight long hair standard of beauty. Wearing dreadlocks is a statement of being proud of their natural hair texture.

WHAT ARE LOCS?

******

Dreadlocks, also known as locs or dreads. Locs are strands of hair formed together by twisting, back combing, rolling or braiding.

Locs are a different way to wear your natural hair, by training your hairs to move in one direction creating a coil around themselves. It can take several months before the hair actually begins to lock.

With the many different textures of hair. The locking method varies. Individuals with a tighter curl pattern will loc quicker with the coil method. An individual with a loose texture pattern may begin to lock their hair from individual braids.

SHOULD I LOCK MY HAIR?

******

Locking your hair is a big decision. Understand that locking your hair is a process and requires a commitment. There are a few things you should think about before beginning your loc journey.

+ Know and understand your hair texture

+ Deciding what loc method is good for your hair texture and lifestyle.

+ Be prepared for the loc journey; the first few months may be frustrating.

+ Wearing your locks at work may be a little messy in the second stage of your loc Journey. Try to keep your edges neat after each wash with healthy styling.

+ When committing to Locs know that you are not limited to one style. Locs are versatile. Your Locs represent you so curl, twist, color and express yourself with your hair.

LOC METHODS

******

There are many ways to begin your locs journey. To begin your loc you need to determine your hair texture, length and lifestyle.

Comb coils – usually used for shorter hair, {that's too short to two-strand twist or braid}. Hair is shampooed, parted and twisted with a comb in one direction to form a coil.

Two strand twists – this is a very popular method throughout the growth process. This method is considered neater than other methods. The hair is sectioned into two and twisted together.

Braids – This method is used for individuals with loose texture hair or hair that does not stay together with coils or twists.

Interlocking – Many of my clients prefer the interlock method. Interlocking requires more work but holds the root locked longer and can be done on any texture hair. A crotches needle or latch hook is used to pull the loc through the root of the hair in 4 directions until the root is pulled together.

Freeform locs – allowing your Locs to form as they please. No maintenance locs will form together creating bigger locs. Though this method is very messy some prefer the untamed look

Backcombing – loose hairs that are pushed back towards your scalp forming a dread. This method is for very fine hair.

LOC STAGES

******

Starter locs

Depending on your loc method this stage will be the beginning of a new hairdo.

Baby locs

Sometimes called sprouting or budding. This stage, your hair might start puffing and become a little frizzy. The puffiness will settle.

Teenage locs

At the teenage stage, your Locs are beginning to find themselves. Some may unravel a little, some may stick up, some may drop. This is the stage to start retightening the base for a neater look.

Some people turn back at the stage because their locs want to do their own thing, but remember it is a process.

******

Mature locs

You should be proud! Your Locs are starting to listen and do what you want them to do, they are thick and are dropping you are beginning to see more growth.

Rooted locs

Congratulations! Your babies have grown into something beautiful your locs are strong and healthy. At this stage, less tightening is needed.

You and your Locs are ready to take on the world embrace and enjoy.

SHAMPOOING YOUR LOCS

******

In the first stage of locking, you want to develop a shampoo routine.

Every 3 to 4 days will allow your hair and scalp to adjust. When shampooing, be gentle, trying not to unravel the hair.

Using a residue-free shampoo can help keep new growth healthy. After establishing a relationship with your new look, you can change your shampoo routine, depending on your scalp condition.
. Using spray leave-in conditioners only is recommended. Using conditioners and creams can cause build up.

Locs can be twisted or interlocked with no products at all. Oil your scalp. A nice blend of natural oils with a good shampoo promotes healthy growth and let your locs do the rest. After your wash squeeze excess water out of your locs. Set aside some time to properly dry your locs.

Letting Locs air dry can cause "Dread Rot" mildew causing a foul odor. Using a hooded dryer or hand dryer is recommended before styling.

LOC MAINTENANCE

******

Do not over twist – Over twisting your locs can lead to thinning at the root.

Be consistent – twist in the same direction. Stick with the same loctician, every stylist is different.

Give your locks a break- styling is nice but to much tension can cause Traction Alopecia. Let your locs hang free.

Loc protection – Protecting your locs is very important. Hair doesn't react very well to extreme heat or cold, especially winter. Investing in silk scarfs and wraps will protect your hair and scalp from drying out.

Breakage – As your locs get longer they may become heavier. They can break at the root if not moisturized often. If your locs begin to think, keep them at a reasonable length to prevent too much weight.

******

Embrace your journey

The lock journey is what you make it. It is a change that allows you to discover new things about you and your hair. From month to month your locs will look different, your length will change. you will feel free and liberated. Embrace the new you. Your locs will be an expression of your self-confidence and inspire others to   join your journey.

Love your locs!

Meet the author

Jasmine Morales, a licensed cosmetologist is married with three children. At a young age through stresses, Jasmine discovered her passion for hair.

Working from home she continued to be teachable, while offering her knowledge to others. While learning and expanding her knowledge for hair. She fell in love with the versatility and beauty of locs.

Opening her first salon in 2011, Jasmine continued to build her clientele; meeting a wide range of different people with different opinions on hair products. She decided to start her own natural hair product line; S.A.J Natural Products.

While striving for her continuous growth and looking at life from a different perspective. She has made it a need to brighten and secure her families future.

LOC

Love 😉

23

Etsy.com/shop/sajnaturalproducts
Instagram; s.a.j._products
Facebook; S.A.J Natural Products

Made in the USA
Thornton, CO
10/19/24 18:38:55

c9f6525b-b49c-4984-b52b-73bf42a0f3aeR01